Interjections Say

"YAY!"

by Michael Dahl

illustrated by Lauren Lowen

PICTURE WINDOW BOOKS
a capstone imprint

2

3

Interjections are words or phrases that can show surprise.

Interjections always show strong feelings.

Interjections can be used during happy times.

9

Interjections can also be used during unhappy times.

Exclamation points love to help interjections.

When you see an interjection in a sentence, an exclamation point is often nearby.

"Interjection" is an interesting word. It comes from the word "interject," which means to squeeze into or between things.

Interjections usually come at the beginning of a sentence.

Sometimes interjections squeeze themselves into the middle of a sentence. They may even come at the end.

Some interjections stand by themselves.

Sounds are often used as interjections.

Adjectives can be interjections too.

Nouns or noun phrases can sometimes be used as interjections.

No matter where interjections are, they always add something extra.

INSPECTING INTERESTING INTERJECTIONS

Interjections help us show strong feelings. (That's why you often see them with exclamation points.)

Wow! This pizza is spicy!

Ick! Your socks are covered in mud!

I did it again! Oops!

D'oh, I forgot my homework!

Some interjections show happy feelings.

Yay, I won free tickets to the cheese museum!

Vacation is finally here! Woohoo!

Some interjections show unhappy feelings.

Ouch! That cactus needle hurts!

A snake is loose in the classroom! Eek!

Because interjections are so helpful, we use them all the time!

Thanks	Oh yeah
Congratulations	Goodbye
No way	Later

ABOUT THE AUTHOR

Michael Dahl is the author of more than 200 books for children and has won the AEP Distinguished Achievement Award three times for his nonfiction. He is the author of the bestselling *Bedtime for Batman* and *You're a Star, Wonder Woman!* picture books. He has written dozens of books of jokes, riddles, and puns. He likes to play with words. In grade school, he read the dictionary for fun. Really. Michael is proud to say that he has always been a noun. A PROPER noun, at that.

ABOUT THE ILLUSTRATOR

Since graduating from the Illustration Department at the Rhode Island School of Design (RISD), **Lauren Lowen** has been creating art for a variety of projects, including publishing, ad campaigns, and products ranging from greeting cards and stickers to activity books and kids' luggage. She taught illustration at both Montserrat College of Art and RISD before becoming an instructor at Watkins College of Art in Nashville, Tennessee, where she currently lives with her husband and son. Some of her favorite things include sushi, chocolate milk, and Star Trek.

GLOSSARY

adjective—a word that tells more about a noun or pronoun

exclamation point—a punctuation mark used to show force or strong feeling

interjection—a word or phrase that shows strong feeling or emotion

noun—a word that names a person, place, or thing

phrase—a group of words that expresses a thought but is not a complete sentence

THINK ABOUT IT

1. What interjections could you use to make the following sentence sound happy or sad? We had broccoli for dinner. Give three examples for each feeling.

2. What interjections could you use to make the following sentence sound angry or scared? The singing birds woke me up this morning. Give three examples for each feeling.

3. Which interjection do you use a lot? Why?

READ MORE

Cleary, Brian P. *Cool! Whoa! Ah and Oh!: What Is an Interjection?* Words Are Categorical. Minneapolis: Millbrook Press, 2011.

Dahl, Michael. *Exclamation Points Say "Wow!"* Word Adventures: Punctuation. North Mankato, MN: Picture Window Books, 2019.

Heinrichs, Ann, and Danielle Jacklin. *Interjections.* Language Rules. New York: AV2 by Weigl, 2018.

INTERNET SITES

Enchanted Learning: Grammar: Interjection
https://www.enchantedlearning.com/grammar/partsofspeech/interjections/index.shtml

Grammaropolis: The Interjections
https://www.grammaropolis.com/interjection.php

Schoolhouse Rock: Interjections
https://www.youtube.com/watch?v=YkAX7Vk3JEw

LOOK FOR ALL THE PARTS OF SPEECH TITLES

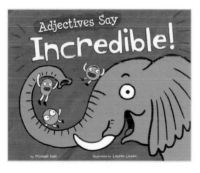

INDEX

Editor: Jill Kalz
Designer: Lori Bye
Production Specialist: Katy LaVigne
The illustrations in this book were created digitally.

Picture Window Books are published by Capstone
1710 Roe Crest Drive, North Mankato, Minnesota 56003
www.capstonepub.com

Library of Congress Cataloging-in-Publication Data is available on the Library of Congress website.
ISBN 978-1-5158-4100-5 (library binding)
ISBN 978-1-5158-4108-1 (paperback)
ISBN 978-1-5158-4104-3 (eBook PDF)
Summary: Hooray! Woohoo! Yay! Sentences and all sorts of pastries get injected with a little sweetness by the playfully illustrated interjection bakers. Informational text flavored with storybook whimsy provides young readers with grammar basics—and plenty of cake. Yum!

All internet sites appearing in back matter were available and accurate when this book was sent to press.

Printed and bound in China.
001654